Cross Stitcher
Magazine's book of
Medieval Designs
IN CROSS STITCH

Cross Stitcher

Magazine's book of

Medieval Designs

IN CROSS STITCH

Steven Jenkins

future
BOOKS

Dedication

To Karen and Gary

First published in 1995 by
Future Books
A division of Future Publishing Limited
30 Monmouth Street, Bath BA1 2BW

Designed by Maria Bowers
Illustrations by Kate Davies
Text by Amanda Cox
Photographic styling by Paula Mabe
Photography by Jonathan Fisher

A catalogue record of this book is available from the British Library

ISBN: 1 85981 045 4

Printed and bound in Malaysia by Times Offset (M) Sdn. Bhd.

CONTENTS

TECHNIQUES

HOW TO PREPARE THE FABRIC

To calculate the amount of fabric you need, add 2in (5cm) all the way round the finished stitched design area, or if it is going to be a framed picture then add 4in (10cm). Make sure that you cut the edges of the fabric straight by following the holes. The fabric should not fray as you stitch or the ends may catch in the stitching. You will also lose the neat edge which will make it difficult to make up or frame the finished piece. There are several ways of ensuring your fabric doesn't fray. A quick and simple method is to fold masking tape around the edges of the fabric. Another method is to stitch the raw edges either by working blanket stitch or overcasting round the edges or by machine with a zigzag stitch. For large pieces of fabric it is best to hem the edges by hand or machine.

HOW TO WORK FROM THE CHARTS

Each symbol on the chart represents one stitch and its position is counted on the fabric using the chart as a guide. Parts of the design may be outlined in back stitch; this is identified by the solid and dotted heavy lines around or through the symbols. The key tells you which symbols represent which colours on the chart and how many strands of thread to use. The pieces are stitched in the threads that are listed in the first column of the key. As the different manufacturer's threads are not exact equivalents, it is advisable to check the colours by eye before you begin stitching if you are going to use a different brand of thread. Other stitches, such as French knots, are listed at the end of the key. We also give details of the finished size that your project will be, so in each case you will have all you need to know.

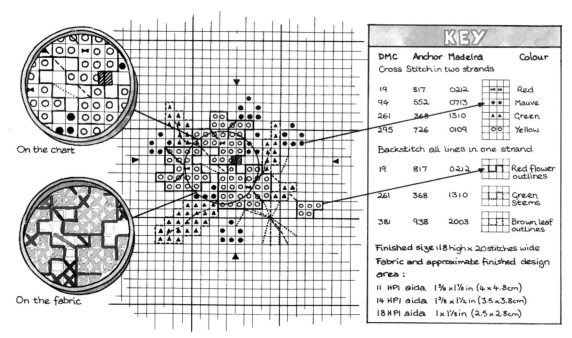

On the chart

On the fabric

KEY

DMC	Anchor	Madeira		Colour
Cross Stitch in two strands				
19	817	0212		Red
94	552	0713		Mauve
261	368	1310		Green
295	726	0109		Yellow
Backstitch all lines in one strand				
19	817	0212		Red flower outlines
261	368	1310		Green stems
381	938	2003		Brown leaf outlines

Finished size : 18 high x 20 stitches wide
Fabric and approximate finished design area :
11 HPI aida 1⅝ x 1⅞ in (4 x 4.8cm)
14 HPI aida 1⅜ x 1½ in (3.5 x 3.8cm)
18 HPI aida 1 x 1⅛ in (2.5 x 2.8cm)

RATINGS

At the beginning of each project you will find two sets of icons. The alarm clocks indicate the approximate time it would take an average stitcher of the suggested skill level to complete the project.

 **1 AN EVENING**

 2 A WEEK

 **3 LESS THAN A MONTH**

4 MORE THAN A MONTH

The skill ratings indicate the level of experience required to stitch the project.

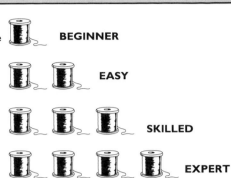 **BEGINNER**

EASY

SKILLED

EXPERT

HOW TO MOUNT FABRIC IN AN EMBROIDERY HOOP

You should use a frame that is suitable for the size of the piece of fabric you are stitching on. It is better to mount your fabric into a hoop or frame as they keep the tension of the stitches even and give the stitching a much neater finish. They also help prevent the fabric from distorting.

There are various different types of hoops and frames available including wooden, plastic and rotating frames. Hoops hold a section of the fabric taut between two rings, and frames keep the entire piece of fabric taut.

If you are using a hoop, place the inner ring of the hoop under the fabric directly below the area you wish to stitch. Loosen the screw on the outer ring and place this over the fabric and inner ring, pushing down over it (illus. 1).

Tighten the screw so that the outer ring fits over the inner ring and fabric, then gently pull the edges of the fabric beyond the hoop so that it is tight. It should be 'drum-tight' when you tap it (illus. 2).

If you want to protect your fabric from the hoop, which is especially important with fine fabrics, wrap fabric tape around the inner ring. Make sure that it overlaps as you wrap it round so that all the ring is covered then fasten it securely at the end by stitching into place.

When using a rotating frame, stitch the edges of the fabric to the end bars then attach the side arms. For a stretcher frame make sure the fabric is positioned centrally over the frame then staple the fabric round the stretcher bars and onto the back, making sure that the fabric is taut.

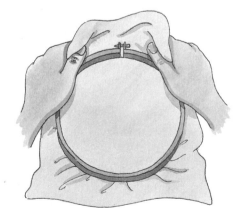

Illustration 1

Illustration 2

HOW TO SIZE YOUR DESIGN

I have given approximate finished design sizes for all the projects but you may want to calculate how big a design will be on a different count fabric. Simply divide the number of stitches on the chart by the number of holes per inch (HPI) of your fabric.

For example, the bluebell design shown is 11 stitches high and 10 stitches wide. If you are stitching on 14 HPI aida you need to calculate the height :

11÷14 = ⅞in (22mm) and the width 10 ÷ 14 = ¾in (19mm).

However, if you are stitching over two threads of the fabric you must divide the HPI by two before calculating the finished design area.

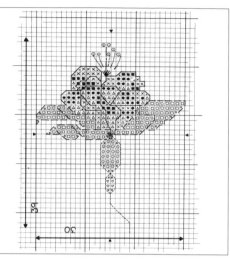

HOW TO WORK CROSS STITCH

Make a full cross stitch for each symbol on the chart. Bring the needle up at 1, down at 2, up at 3 and down at 4.

If you are working a block of stitches of the same colour, first work all the half stitches in one direction. Turn and work back along the row completing all the crosses.

HOW TO STITCH OVER TWO THREADS

If you are working on a high count fabric such as 28 HPI evenweave or linen, it is usual to stitch over two threads of the fabric. This will give the same finished design area as 14 HPI aida. Likewise, if you are working on 36 HPI linen you will get the same area as 18 HPI aida. Make each stitch cross over two threads to cover a nine hole square instead of the usual four hole square.

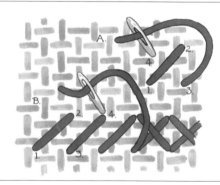

HOW TO STITCH BACK STITCH

Follow the solid or dotted lines for the back stitch using the number of strands which are indicated in the key.

Make the first stitch from left to right. Pass the needle behind the fabric, and bring it out one stitch length ahead to the left. Repeat and continue along the line in this way.

HOW TO STITCH FRENCH KNOTS

Bring the needle up where you want the knot to be. Hold the thread where it comes out of the fabric with your left hand. For a small knot, twist the needle round the thread once; for a large knot, twist it round two or three times. Holding the thread taut, push the needle down into the fabric close to where it emerged.

When the needle is halfway through the fabric, tighten the thread close up to the needle to form a knot. Continue pushing the needle and thread back to the wrong side of the fabric.

HOW TO STITCH THREE-QUARTER AND QUARTER STITCH

If there is a symbol in the corner of a square, you should make a three-quarter stitch in that position. The symbol will be a smaller version of the full stitch symbol shown in the key. First, work a quarter stitch by bringing the needle up at that corner and pushing it down in the centre then stitch the diagonal half stitch across it. If you are working over one thread such as with 14 HPI aida then you will have to split the threads in the centre.

Where two different symbols share a square on the chart, one is a three-quarter stitch in one colour and one is a quarter stitch in another colour. It is up to you which colour you choose to be the main colour, but it is better if the three-quarter stitch is in the colour you want to be more prominent.

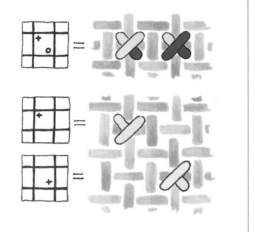

FRENCH KNOTS (continued)

If you are left-handed, hold the needle in your left hand and the thread in your right. Twist the needle clockwise round the thread. Keeping the thread in your right hand, insert the needle into the fabric to the left of the original hole where the thread emerged and pull up the thread in order to tighten the knot. Push the needle through the fabric.

HOW TO STITCH BLANKET STITCH

Blanket stitch is used mainly for edging projects - such as bookmarks and table settings. It is a very useful stitch, but care needs to be taken to keep the stitches even. Blanket stitch is worked from left to right. Bring the needle up at 1, then insert it above and slightly to the right at point 2. Bring the needle up again at point 3, below and to the right of point 1, with the thread under the needle. Finally, pull the needle through the fabric to form a right angle.

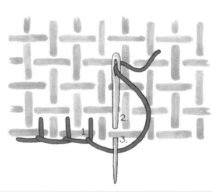

HOW TO WASH YOUR FINISHED STITCHING

If you notice any marks on your finished work, you can wash it. Immerse the stitched piece in luke-warm water. If the colours start to run, don't worry, just keep rinsing until the water runs clear. If there are any stubborn stains, rub a little detergent on to the area until the stain is removed.

● Roll the wet fabric in a towel to remove excess water.

● Pad your ironing board with a thick, clean, white towel. Place your work right side down on this with a thin clean cloth over it. Press carefully until the fabric is dry. The thickness of the towel will prevent you from flattening the stitches.

Iron into the stitches with the point of the iron in a circular motion - this will raise the stitches and improve their appearance. Be carfeul to avoid having the iron too hot or pressing too hard.

HOW TO MOUNT YOUR WORK IN A SMALL FRAME

Should you wish to mount your work in a small frame, hold the frame in both hands, pushing out the clear plastic and snap-in plastic back, with your thumbs.

Place the clear plastic centrally over your stitched fabric and draw round it with a pencil. Cut a piece of light-weight iron-on interfacing slightly larger than the clear plastic then iron it on the back of the stitching.

Cut round the pencil line. If you want to pad your work and not place the clear plastic front inside then cut a piece of 2 oz. wadding the same size as the fabric.

Place the stitched fabric then the wadding into the frame. Finally push the plastic back behind them into the frame. If you want to use the clear plastic front put this in first then the stitching and finally the plastic back to complete.

HOW TO LACE YOUR WORK FOR FRAMING

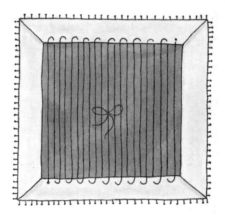

Illustration 1

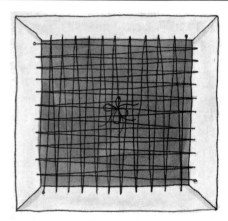

Illustration 2

Cut a piece of acid free mount board to the same size as the inside of the frame. This will be your lacing board.

If you want to use a coloured mount inside your frame then cut a piece of 2oz. wadding to the same size as the mount opening. If you are not using a mount then cut the wadding to the size of the frame opening. Place the wadding centrally on the lacing board.

Centre your stitched fabric right side up over the wadding and lacing board. Push pins through the fabric and into the board along the top edge. Use the holes of the fabric as a guide to ensure that you pin it straight.

Pull the fabric gently and pin along the bottom in the same way. Repeat this for the other two sides.

Working from the back of the board, thread a large-eyed needle with thick strong cotton such as crochet cotton and tie a knot at the end. Lace from top to bottom using an under and over motion. Stop halfway across the back and repeat the lacing for the other side. When you reach the centre, go back and remove the slack from the threads by pulling them tightly one by one. Once you have done this, knot the two ends at the centre.

Repeat this process from side to side. If at any stage you run out of thread before you reach the centre, join a new piece with a reef knot.

Fold in the corners and stitch into place then remove the pins. Your work is now ready to be framed (illus. 2).

HOW TO MOUNT YOUR STITCHING INTO A CARD

Place strips of double sided tape on the inside of B at the edges of the card.

Place your finished design face upwards on the table. Turn your card over and hold it centrally above the stitched design. Press the card down on the table until it holds firmly.

Turn the card over so that it is face down with the base of the design towards you. Place strips of double sided tape on the outside edges of A. Place the wadding over the back of the stitched fabric and press down A onto B, making sure that the wadding stays in place as you do this.

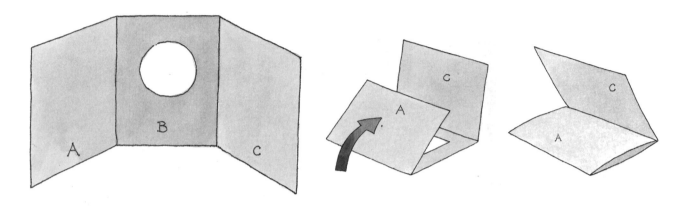

HOW TO FRAME YOUR PICTURE

Place the glass from the frame centrally over your finished stitching and draw round it with a pencil.

Place the interfacing centrally over the back of the stitching and iron it on making sure that the iron is not too hot.

Cut out the fabric and interfacing around the pencil line. Cut the wadding to the same size.

Place the fabric into the frame with the wadding and frame back behind it. If you want to use the glass then this should be put in before the stitched fabric.

If you prefer, you can mount your design in a card mount (see above).

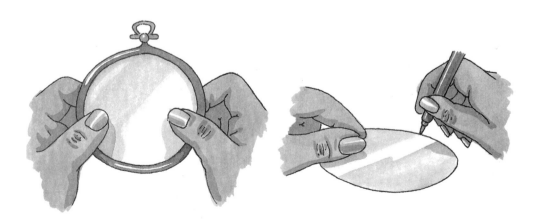

HOW TO MAKE A CUSHION COVER

CUT THE FABRIC INTO THE FOLLOWING SIZES:

2 strips 16x4in (40.6x10.2cm) - for the borders (top and bottom)
2 strips 10x4in (25.4x10.2cm) - for the borders (left and right sides)
1 piece 16x16in (40.6x40.6cm) - for the back

INSTRUCTIONS

Pin one of the shorter border strips right sides together to the top edge of the stitched canvas, making sure that it is placed centrally. Stitch the fabric to the aida using a ½in (13mm) seam allowance. You will find it easier to achieve a straight line if you stitch with the aida facing upwards and stitch through the holes. Stitch the other short strip to the bottom of the aida (illus. 1). Make sure that you press the seams as you go along as this will give you a neater and more accurate finish. Then pin and stitch the long strips on to each side of this piece matching up the edges. This will give you a square 16x16in (40.6x40.6cm).

Place the front and back of the cushion cover together, right sides together, and pin all the way around the edge.

Using a ½in (13mm) seam allowance, stitch the two pieces together leaving a 10in (25.4cm) opening along one side (illus. 2).

Turn the cover right sides out and insert the cushion pad. Using small slip stitches, close up the seam.

FOR THE CHALICE CUSHION

Hand stitch the cord to the completed cushion, laying it on the seam line and using matching thread and a small curved needle (this makes it easier to get through the fabric). Make small stitches through the fabric and the underside of the cord so that your stitching will not be seen from the top (illus. 3).

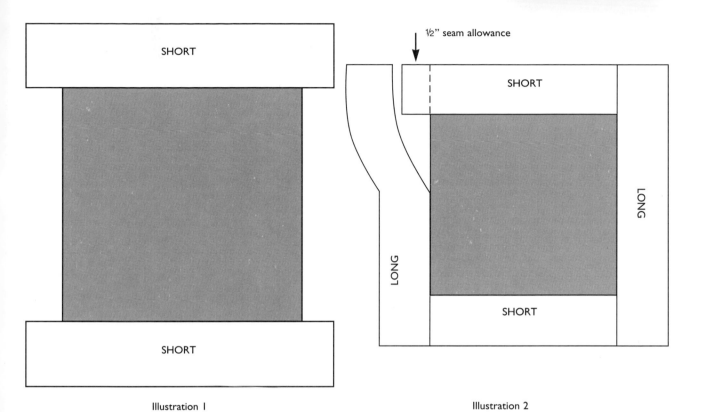

SHORT

SHORT

Illustration 1

½" seam allowance

SHORT

LONG

LONG

SHORT

Illustration 2

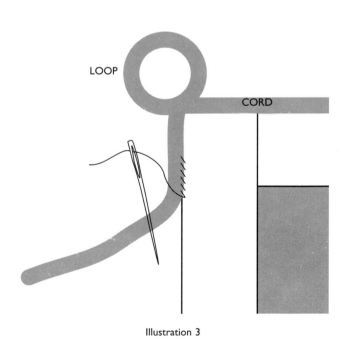

LOOP

CORD

Illustration 3

PIN CUSHION

Make this stylish and evocative
pin cushion as an invaluable
aid to all your stitching projects.

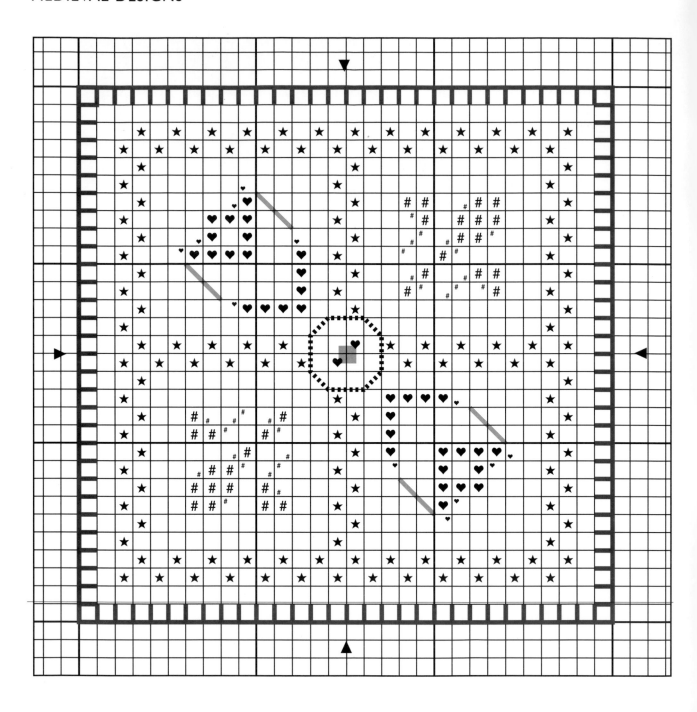

YOU WILL NEED

- **14 HPI aida - 3¼x6in (8.3x15.2cm), dark blue**
- **Stranded cotton - as listed in the key**
- **Metallic thread - Madeira metallic gold No.12 - 33 Gold**
- **Tapestry needle - size 24**
- **2oz wadding (for filling)**

Did you know that the world 'medieval' comes from the Latin *medium aevum* meaning the Middle Ages? It spans the thousand years from about 500 to 1500.

PIN CUSHION KEY

ANCHOR	DMC	MADEIRA		COLOUR
Cross stitch in two strands				
047	321	0510	♥♥	Red
227	701	1305	★★	Green
Madeira metallic gold No.12 33			##	Gold
Backstitch in two strands				
047	321	0510		Red design detail
227	701	1305		Green design detail
Blanket stitch in one strand				
047	321	0510		Red edging detail

Our model was stitched using Anchor threads; the DMCand Madeira conversions are not necessarily exact colour equivalents.

Finished size: Stitch count 30 high x 30 wide
Fabric and approximate finished design area:
11HPI aida 23/4x23/4ins
14HPI aida21/8x21/8ins
18HPI aida13/4x13/4ins

HOW TO STITCH

It is best to start stitching from the centre - this ensures an even amount of fabric all round the design. Find the centre of your fabric by folding it lightly in half both ways. The centre of the chart is indicated by a grey square.

Work the cross stitch first using two strands of either stranded cotton or metallic thread where indicated.

When you have completed the cross stitch, you can work the following backstitch in two strands: red on red motif and green around the centre.

Once the stitching is complete, trim the fabric to 2¼x4½in(5.7x11.4cm) making sure that you leave at least two squares around the stitched design. Fold the fabric in half wrong sides together. Using one strand of red, blanket stitch around two raw edges and the fold of the fabric to form a pocket. Insert the wadding taking care not to overfill, and complete your blanket stitching along the open edge to finish off.

MEDIEVAL KING

Bring the regal splendour of the Middle Ages into your home with this magnificent king's head stained glass window design.

YOU WILL NEED

- 28 HPI evenweave 14x17in (35.6x43.2cm), cream
- Stranded cotton - as listed in the key
- Tapestry needle - size 24
- Frame - 6½x10in (16.5x25.4cm), gilt finish
- Mount - cut to the shape of the design allowing ¼in around it, green
- 2oz wadding - cut to the shape of the design allowing ¼in around it

MEDIEVAL KING KEY

ANCHOR	DMC	MADEIRA		COLOUR
Cross stitch in two strands				
188	943	1114	◆◆	Dark green
239	702	1306	●●	Green
298	972	0107	◎◎	Yellow
335	606	0209	♥♥	Red
373	3046	2103	××	Beige
Backstitch in one strand				
403	310	Black		Black king's facial and costume details and outlines
Backstitch in two strands				
239	702	1306		Green window details

Our model was stitched using Anchor threads; the DMC and Madeira conversions are not necessarily exact colour equivalents.

Finished size: Stitch count 100 high x 56 wide
Fabric and approximate finished design area:
11HPI aida 9⅛x5⅛in
18HPI aida 5⅝x3⅛in
28HPI evenweave 7⅛x4in

HOW TO STITCH

It is best to start stitching from the centre - this ensures an even amount of fabric all round the design. Find the centre of your fabric by folding it lightly in half both ways. The centre of the chart is indicated by a grey square.

Work the cross stitch first using two strands of stranded cotton.

When you have completed the cross stitch, you can work the backstitch. Use one strand of black for the outlines and details on the king's face, beard, hair and costume and two strands of green for the detailing on the window behind him.

Once the stitching is complete, you can wash and prepare your work for framing following the instructions on the technique pages at the beginning of the book.

The legend of King Arthur and the Knights of the Round Table originated as early as 1136. He became the embodiment of the ideal Christian Knight. A knight would take the vows of chivalry: 'to fear God, serve the king, protect the weak and live honourably'. The word 'chivalry' comes from the French *chevalier*, meaning knight.

GOTHIC TOWER

The glory of medieval architecture is reincarnated in this handsome design, which looks great framed or sewn onto a cushion.

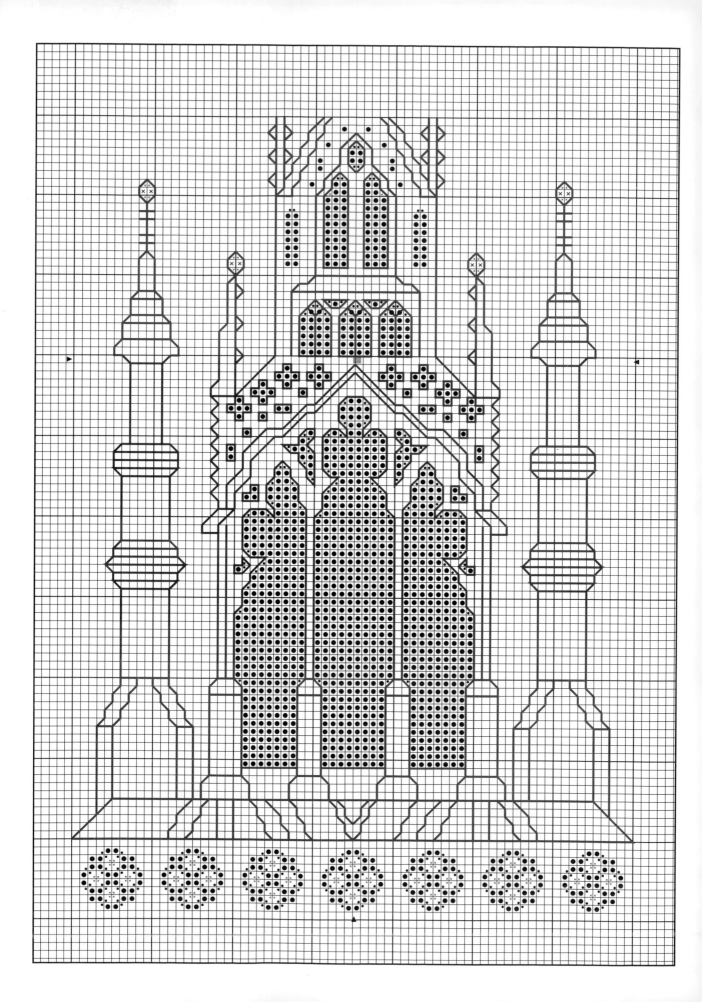

YOU WILL NEED

- 14 HPI aida - 12x18in (30.5x45.7cm), red
- Stranded cotton - as listed in the key
- Metallic thread - Madeira metallic gold No.12 - 33 Gold
- Tapestry needle - size 24
- Frame - 7½x12½in (19x31.8cm) gilt finish
- Mount - with a 5½x10½in (14x26.7cm) opening
- 2oz wadding - 5½x10½in (14x26.7cm)

GOTHIC TOWER KEY

ANCHOR	DMC	MADEIRA		COLOUR
Cross stitch in two strands				
1218	501	1205	● ●	Green
Cross stitch in three strands				
Madeira metallic gold No.12 33			x x	Gold
Backstitch in two strands				
Madeira metallic gold No.12 33				Gold tower outlines and details

Our model was stitched using Anchor threads; the DMC and Madeira conversions are not necessarily exact colour equivalents.

Finished size: Stitch count 140 high x 70 wide
Fabric and approximate finished design area:
11HPI aida 12¾x6⅜in
14HPI aida 10x5in
18HPI aida 7¾x3⅞in

HOW TO STITCH

It is best to start stitching from the centre - this ensures an even amount of fabric all round the design. Find the centre of your fabric by folding it lightly in half both ways. The centre of the chart is indicated by a grey square.

Work the cross stitch first using two strands of stranded cotton. Use three strands of metallic thread in this design.

When you have completed the cross stitch, you can work the following backstitch in two strands of metallic thread: gothic tower outlines and details.

Once the stitching is complete, you can wash and prepare your work for framing following the instructions in the technique pages at the beginning of the book.

TOP OF THE TOWER

JEWELLED CHALICE

Reminiscent of ceremonial banquets in great stone halls, this ornate goblet will add style to a cushion or will brighten any dining room wall.

YOU WILL NEED

- 14 HPI aida - 12½x12½in (31.8x31.8cm), green
- Stranded cotton - as listed in the key
- Metallic thread - Madeira metallic gold No.12 - 33 Gold
- Tapestry needle - size 24
- Fabric for the cushion - ½ yard (45.5cm) - green
- Gold braid - 2 yds (1½ metres)
- Matching thread - for making up cushion
- White pencil
- Usual sewing kit - including sharp needle, pins, scissors, etc.
- Cushion pad - 15x15in (38x38cm)

JEWELLED CHALICE KEY

ANCHOR	DMC	MADEIRA		COLOUR
Cross stitch in two strands				
112	552	0713	■■	Purple
306	725	0113	⊙⊗	Dull gold
307	783	2212	◆•	Brass
309	781	2213	●●	Dark brass
334	606	0209	♥♥	Red
Madeira metallic gold No.12 33			★★	Gold
Backstitch in one strand				
403	310	Black		Black chalice details
Madeira metallic gold No.12 33				Gold chalice details

Our model was stitched using Anchor threads; the DMC and Madeira conversions are not necessarily exact colour equivalents.

Finished size: Stitch count 99 high x 75 wide
Fabric and approximate finished design area:
11HPI aida 9x6⅞in	**14HPI** aida 7⅛x5⅜in
18HPI aida 5½x4⅛in	

HOW TO STITCH

It is best to start stitching from the centre - this ensures an even amount of fabric all round the design. Find the centre of your fabric by folding it lightly in half both ways. The centre of the chart is indicated by a grey square.

Work the cross stitch first using two strands of stranded cotton. Use three strands of the metallic thread in this design where indicated.

When you have completed the cross stitch, you can work the following backstitch: one strand of black stranded cotton for the chalice rims, jewel outlines and other details; three strands of metallic thread for detail and patterning on the chalice.

Once the stitching is complete, you can wash and prepare your work to make it into a cushion.

The Holy Grail, the object of the most famous quest of King Arthur and his Knights of the Round Table, was reputed to be the chalice from which Jesus drank at the Last Supper, before the Crucifixion.

HERALDIC UNICORN

Mythical beast and symbol of pageantry, the unicorn held a special place in medieval folklore and makes a fine framed decoration in the modern home.

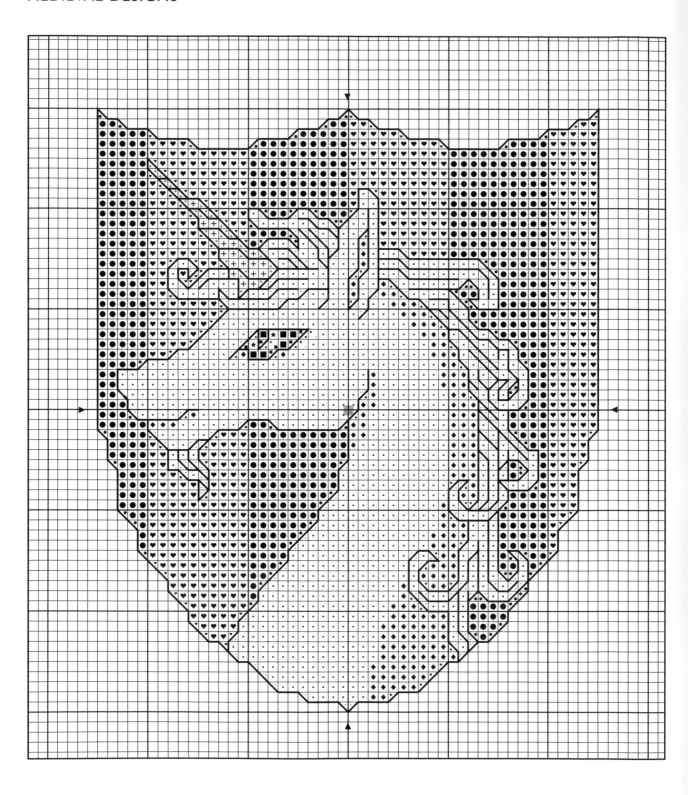

YOU WILL NEED

- 14 HPI aida - 10x11in (25.4x27.9cm), stone
- Stranded cotton - as listed in the key
- Madeira Metallic thread No.12 - 33 Gold
- Tapestry needle - size 24
- Wooden box (from 'Remember When')

HERALDIC UNICORN KEY

ANCHOR	DMC	MADEIRA		COLOUR
Cross stitch in two strands				
001	White	White		White
047	321	0510		Red
133	796	0913		Blue
349	301	2306		Brown
403	310	Black		Black
848	927	1708		Light blue
Madeira metallic gold No.12	33			Gold
Backstitch in one strand				
403	310	Black		Black shield outline, unicorn outline and details

Our model was stitched using Anchor threads; the DMC and Madeira conversions are not necessarily exact colour equivalents.

Finished size: Stitch count 60 high x 50 wide
Fabric and approximate finished design area:
11HPI aida 5½x4½in
14HPI aida 4¼x3⅝in
18HPI aida 3⅜x2¾in

HOW TO STITCH

It is best to start stitching from the centre - this ensures an even amount of fabric all round the design. Find the centre of your fabric by folding it lightly in half both ways. The centre of the chart is indicated by a grey square.

Work the cross stitch first using two strands of stranded cotton.

Once the stitching is complete, you can wash and prepare your work for mounting. The finished piece can be mounted onto the box as shown in the technique pages.

The unicorn is a mythical and heraldic beast first described in 400 BC by Ctesias. It was believed that by dipping its horn into a liquid, the unicorn could detect whether or not it was poisoned.

TILE COASTERS

These decorative tile coasters make a neat little gift and will add a touch of evocative flair to any dinner table.

YOU WILL NEED

- You will need:
- 14 HPI aida - 5x5ins (12.7x12.7cm), cream
- Stranded cotton - as listed in the key
- Tapestry needle - size 24

TILE COASTERS KEY

ANCHOR	DMC	MADEIRA		COLOUR
Cross stitch in two strands				
133	796	0913	●●	Blue
306	725	0113	··	Light orange
326	720	0309	■■	Dark orange
Backstitch in two strands				
133	796	0913	●●	Blue coaster edging
306	725	0113	■■	Light orange coaster edging

Finished size Tile 1 - 56x56 stitches
Finished size Tile 2 - 57x57 stitches

Our model was stitched using Anchor threads; the DMC and Madeira conversions are not necessarily exact colour equivalents.

Finished size of Coaster 1 (Tile): Stitch count 56 high x 56 wide
Fabric and approximate finished design area:
11HPI aida 5⅛x5⅛in
14HPI aida 4x4in
18HPI aida 3⅛x3⅛in

Finished size of Coaster 2 (Bird): Stitch count 57 high x 57 wide
Fabric and approximate finished design area:
11HPI aida 5⅛x5⅛in
14HPI aida 4x4in
18HPI aida 3⅛x3⅛in

HOW TO STITCH

It is best to start stitching from the centre - this ensures an even amount of fabric all round the design. Find the centre of your fabric by folding it lightly in half both ways. The centre of the chart is indicated by a grey square.

Work the cross stitch first using two strands of stranded cotton.

When you have completed the cross stitch, backstitch around the stitched piece in two strands of light orange for the bird; blue for the tile design, to give a firm edge.

Once the stitching is complete, trim the fabric to leave four squares of unstitched fabric right round the design. Carefully remove the loose threads to produce a decorative frayed effect.

The griffin is a fabulous beast of mythology fabled to be the offspring of the lion and the eagle. It has the legs, head and shoulders of an eagle; the rest of the body is that of a lion. It is sacred to the sun and keeps guard over hidden treasures.

MANUSCRIPT SAMPLER

Stitch this superb medieval
alphabet to make a resplendent
wall mounting or the new cover
of a cherished old book.

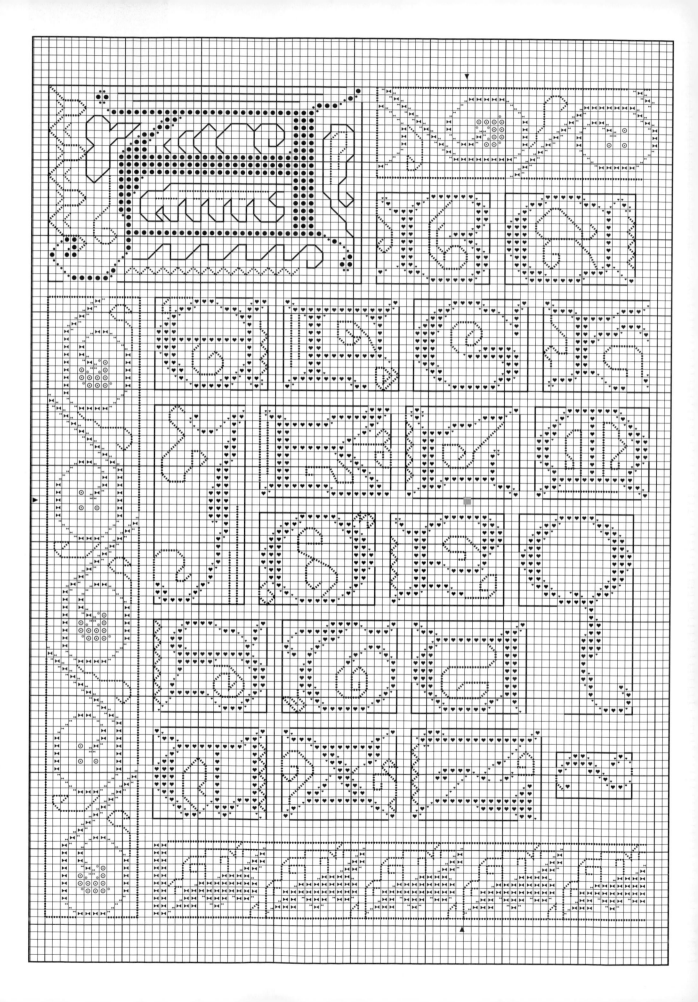

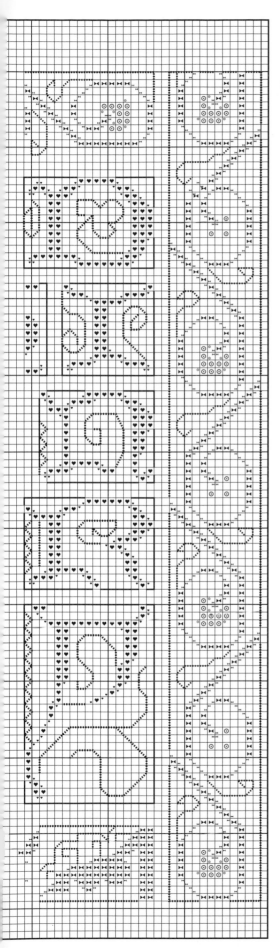

MANUSCRIPT SAMPLER KEY

ANCHOR	DMC	MADEIRA		COLOUR
Cross stitch in two strands				
047	321	0510		Red
143	797	0912		Blue
227	701	1305		Green
291	444	0106		Yellow
Backstitch in two strands				
047	321	0510		Red lettering detail
143	797	0912		Blue lettering detail
227	701	1305		Green lettering detail

Our model was stitched using Anchor threads; the DMC and Madeira conversions are not necessarily exact colour equivalents.

Finished size: Stitch count 109 high x 110 wide
Fabric and approximate finished design area:
11HPI aida 10x10in   14HPI aida 7⅞x7⅞in
18HPI aida 6⅛x6⅛in

HOW TO STITCH

It is best to start stitching from the centre - this ensures an even amount of fabric all round the design. Find the centre of your fabric by folding it lightly in half both ways. The centre of the chart is indicated by a grey square.

Work the cross stitch first using two strands of stranded cotton.

When you have completed the cross stitch, you can work the lettering detail in backstitch using two strands of either red, blue and green, using the different backstitch styles as indicated on the chart as your guide.

Once the stitching is complete, you can wash and prepare your work for framing following the instructions in the technique pages at the beginning of the book.

YOU WILL NEED

- 14 HPI aida - 15x15in (38.1x38.1cm), cream
- Stranded cotton - as listed in the key
- Tapestry needle - size 24
- Frame - 8½x8½in (21.6x21.6cm), medium wood with gilt trim
- 2oz wadding - 8½x8½in (21.6x21.6 cm)

ROSE WINDOW

The colour and luminescence of
this beautiful rose window will
bring the majesty of a Gothic
cathedral into your home.

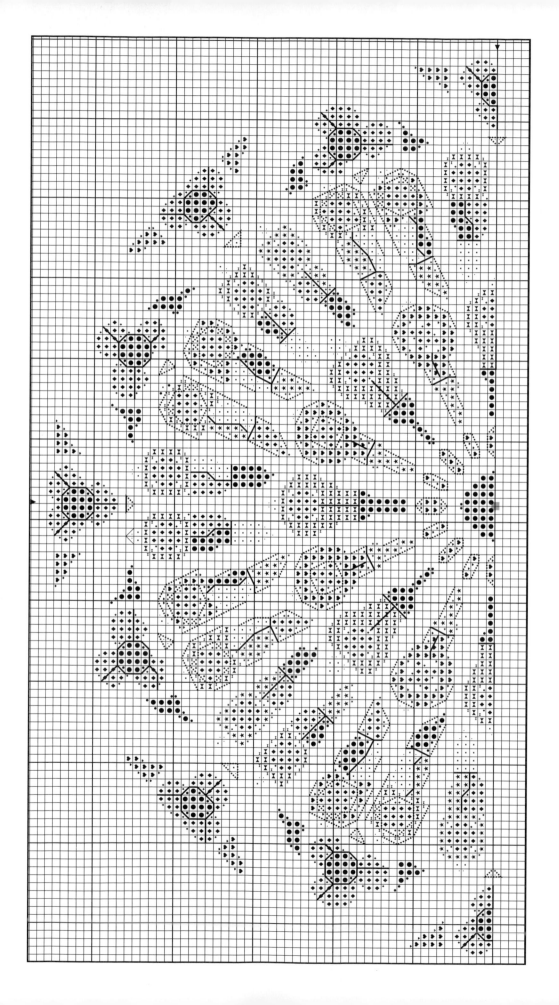

YOU WILL NEED

- You will need:
- 14 HPI aida - black 12x12in (30.5x30.5cm)
- Stranded cotton - as listed in the key
- Tapestry needle - size 24
- Blue furnishing fabric for making up cushion - ½ yd (45.7cm)
- Matching thread - for cushion
- Usual sewing kit - including sharp needle, pins, scissors, etc.
- Cushion pad - 15x15in (38x38cm)

ROSE WINDOW KEY

ANCHOR	DMC	MADEIRA		COLOUR
Cross stitch in two strands				
001	White	White	· ·	White
047	321	0510	♥ ♥	Red
133	796	0913	● ●	Medium blue
291	444	0106	♦ ♦	Yellow
433	996	1103	⋈ ⋈	Light blue
923	909	1303	★ ★	Green
Backstitch in two strands				
403	310	Black		Black stained glass detail
Outline in self colour				Individual stained glass segments

Our model was stitched using Anchor threads; the DMC and Madeira conversions are not necessarily exact colour equivalents.

Finished size: Stitch count 112 high x 112 wide
Fabric and approximate finished design area:
11HPI aida 10⅛x10⅛in
14HPI aida 8x8in
18HPI aida 6¼x6¼in

HOW TO STITCH

It is best to start stitching from the centre - this ensures an even amount of fabric all round the design. Find the centre of your fabric by folding it lightly in half both ways. The centre of the chart is indicated by a grey square.

Work the cross stitch first using two strands of stranded cotton.

When you have completed the cross stitch, you can work the backstitch. Use two strands of black for the stained glass window detail. The separate coloured panes are outlined in two strands of the same colour (referred to as 'self colour' in the key).

Once the stitching is complete, you can wash and prepare your work for mounting as a cushion cover following the instructions in the technique pages at the beginning of the book.

Stained glass was produced by adding metals to glass in a liquid state to create beautiful colours and designs. The Gothic cathedral of Notre Dame in Paris has a magnificent stained glass rose window design.

WALL HANGING

If you are looking to fill a vacant space in a corner or window bay, what better than this *fleur de lys* and other classic medieval designs on a wall hanging?

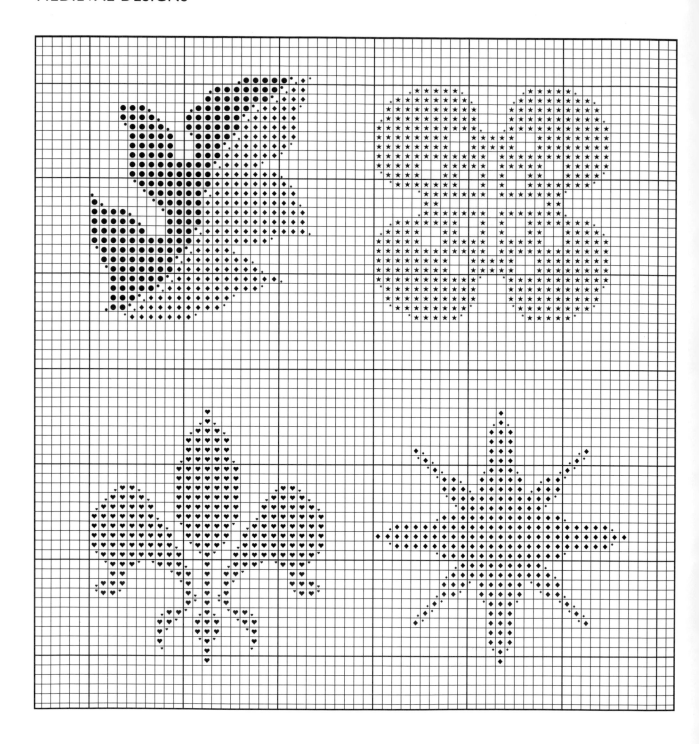

The *Fleur-de-lys* is the heraldic lily, historically belonging to the old French royal family.

WALL HANGING KEY

ANCHOR	DMC	MADEIRA		COLOUR
Cross stitch in two strands				
Leaf Motif				
227	701	1305	●●	Green
291	444	0106	◆◆	Yellow
Emblem Motif				
Madeira metallic gold No.12		33	★★	Gold
Fleur de lis Motif				
047	321	0510	♥♥	Red
Sun Motif				
291	444	0106	◆◆	Yellow

Our model was stitched using Anchor threads; the DMC and Madeira conversions are not necessarily exact colour equivalents.

Finished size: Stitch count 27 high x 27 wide (max)
Fabric and approximate finished design area:
11HPI aida 2½x2½in
14HPI aida 2x2 in
18HPI aida 1½x1½in

HOW TO STITCH

We have stitched the motifs as a wallhanging, leaving twelve squares at each end and twelve squares in between each one. You can adapt the design, by repeating just one, or arranging them in a different layout.

It is best to start stitching from the centre of each motif - this ensures an even amount of fabric all round the design. Find the centre of your fabric by folding it lightly in half both ways. The centre of the chart is indicated by a grey square.

Work the cross stitch using two strands of stranded cotton.

Once the stitching is complete, turn under six squares along the sides and hem carefully with small, neat stitches. Turn under four squares top and bottom to neaten the edges. Fold over 1½in (3.8cm) and stitch a seam one inch (2.5cm) from the fold to leave a space to thread through the wallhanging poles if required.

MEDIEVAL QUEEN

The queen can be united with her king, in a perfect framed set, if you stitch this elegant design full of ancient mystique.

52

YOU WILL NEED

- 28 HPI evenweave 14x17in (35.6x43.2cm), cream
- Stranded cotton - as listed in the key
- Tapestry needle - size 24
- Frame - 6½x10in (16.5x25.4cm), gilt finish
- Mount - cut to the shape of the design allowing ¼in around it, green
- 2oz wadding - cut to the shape of the design allowing ¼in around it

MEDIEVAL QUEEN KEY

ANCHOR	DMC	MADEIRA		COLOUR
Cross stitch in two strands				
008	353	0304	⌐⌐	Pink
188	943	1114	●●	Dark green
239	702	1306	►◄	Green
298	972	0107	⊙⊙	Yellow
335	606	0209	♥♥	Red
373	3046	2103	××	Beige
Backstitch in one strand				
239	702	1306		Green window details
403	310	Black		Black queen's facial and costume outlines and details

Our model was stitched using Anchor threads; the DMC and Madeira conversions are not necessarily exact colour equivalents.

Finished size: Stitch count 100 high x 56 wide
Fabric and approximate finished design area:
11HPI aida 9⅛x5⅛in
18HPI aida 5⅝x3⅛in
28HPI evenweave 7⅛x4in

HOW TO STITCH

It is best to start stitching from the centre - this ensures an even amount of fabric all round the design. Find the centre of your fabric by folding it lightly in half both ways. The centre of the chart is indicated by a grey square.

Work the cross stitch first using two strands of stranded cotton.

When you have completed the cross stitch, you can work the backstitch. Use one strand of black for the outlines and details on the queen's face, hair and costume and one strand of green for the detailing on the window behind her.

Once the stitching is complete, you can wash and prepare your work for framing following the instructions in the technique pages at the beginning of the book.

Travelling story-tellers called 'jongleurs' were extremely popular throughout the Middle Ages and went from court to court with their tales of courtly love and chivalry. Many of these have been passed down to us today, including the tragic romance of Queen Guinevere and Lancelot.

Acknowledgements

The Publishers would like to thank the following people for their help in creating this book:

Tracy Medway and Sheila Wheeler for stitching the designs

The Kit Company for framing and supplying kits

For supplying props for photography:
Papyrus, Bath (pages 26, 42)
Past Times, Bath (pages 18, 26, 38, 46)
Phillips, Bath (pages 26, 50)
Staks, Bath (page 26)
Villa Mimosa, Bath (page 26, 50)

Thanks are also due to Anchor Threads for supplying fabric and threads

For kindly allowing location photography:
Charlcombe Church (page 42)
St John the Baptist Church, Colerne, Wilts (pages 18, 38, 46)

SUPPLIERS

For information on your nearest stockist of embroidery cotton, contact the following:

COATS AND ANCHOR

UK
Kilncraigs Mill
Alloa
Clackmannanshire
Scotland FK10 1EG

USA
Coats & Clark
P.O. Box 27067
Dept. CO1
Greenville
SC 29616

AUSTRALIA
Coats Patons Crafts
Thistle Street
Launceston
Tasmania
7250

DMC

UK
DMC Creative World Limited
62 Pullman Road
Wigston
Leicester LE8 2DY

USA
The DMC Corporation
Port Kearney Blc.
10 South Kearney
N.J. 07032-0650

AUSTRALIA
DMC Needlecraft Pty
P.O. Box 317
Earlswood 2206
NSW 2204

MADEIRA

UK
Madeira Threads (UK) Limited
Thirsk Industrial Park
York Road
Thirsk
North Yorkshire YO7 3BX

USA
Madeira Marketing Limited
600 East 9th Street
Michigan City
IN 46360

AUSTRALIA
Penguin Threads Pty Limited
25-27 Izett Street
Prahran
Victoria 3181

XXXXX

LIST OF TITLES IN THE SERIES

Country Animals in Cross Stitch
Country Flowers in Cross Stitch
Medieval Designs in Cross Stitch
Teddy Bears in Cross Stitch

FURTHER READING FROM FUTURE BOOKS

Future Books publish a growing range of stitching titles which may be of interest to readers of this book. In addition to the series listed above, the following titles are also available:

Cross Stitcher Magazine's Country Keepsakes - 50 Delightful Cross Stitch Designs
The Needlecraft Magazine Book of Embroidery Stitches
The Needlecraft Magazine Book of Needlepoint Stitches

For further information, contact
The Publisher
Future Books
Future Publishing Limited
30 Monmouth Street
Bath
BA1 2BW